Port Salerno

Salerno Sewer

Project Vision and History

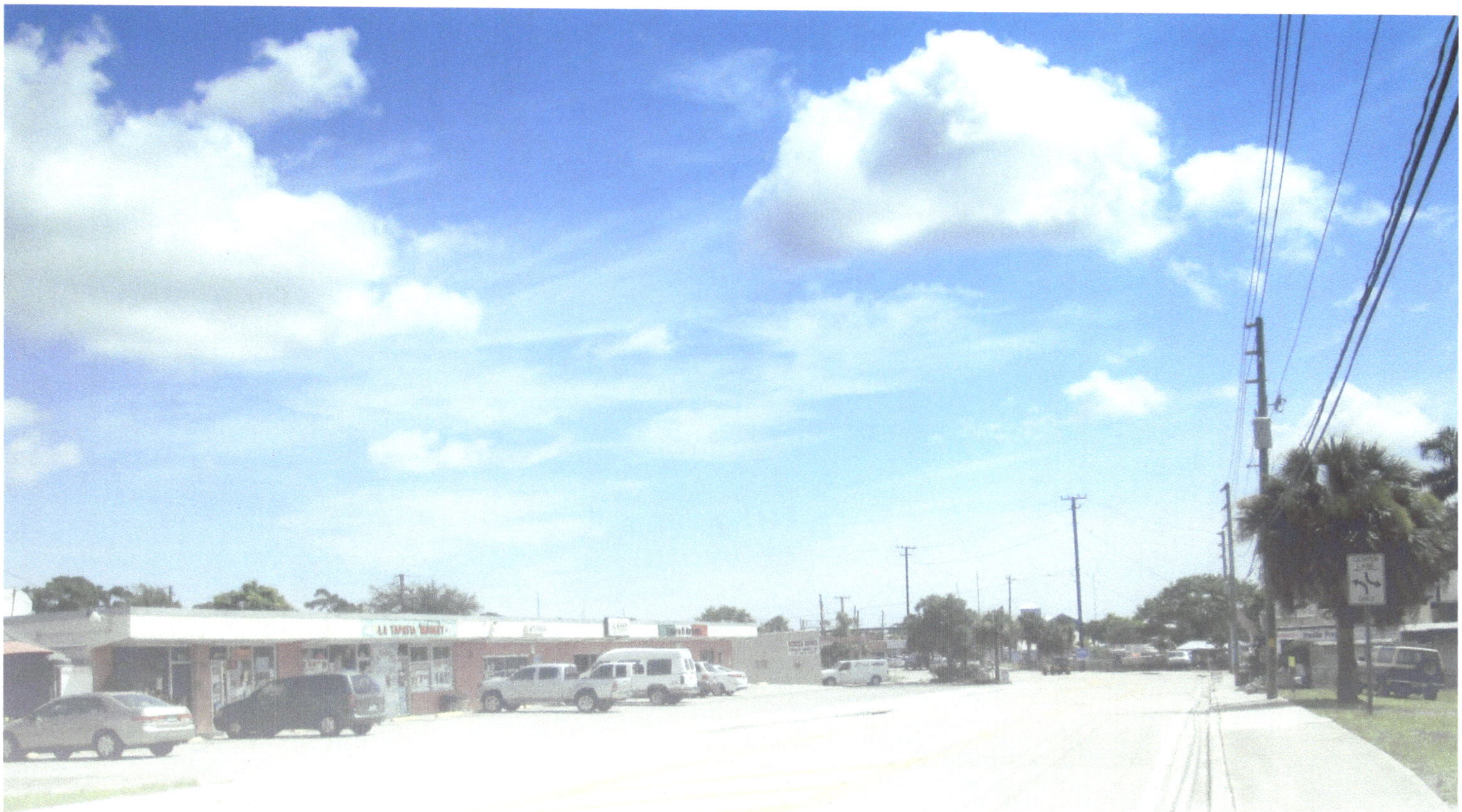

Community Development Department

Martin County Administrative Center
2401 S.E. Monterey Road
Stuart, Florida 34996
(772) 288-5497

MARTIN COUNTY
Community Redevelopment Agency

Dynamic   Innovative   Sustainable

MARTIN COUNTY
Community Redevelopment Agency

MARTIN COUNTY BOARD OF COUNTY COMMISSIONERS

District 1	Doug Smith
District 2	Ed Fielding, Chair
District 3	Ann Scott, Vice Chair
District 4	Sarah Heard
District 5	John Haddox

MARTIN COUNTY
Community Redevelopment Agency

MARTIN COUNTY COMMUNITY REDEVELOPMENT AGENCY

District 1	Doug Smith
District 2	Ed Fielding, Chair
District 3	Ann Scott, Vice Chair
District 4	Sarah Heard
District 5	John Haddox

COMMUNITY DEVELOPMENT STAFF

Kev Freeman, Director
Edward Erfurt, Urban Designer
Nancy Johnson, Community Development Specialist
Nakeischea Smith, AICP, Community Development Specialist
Pinal Gandhi-Savdas, Community Development Specialist

Dynamic   Innovative   Sustainable

salerno road
Corridor Improvements

MARTIN COUNTY
Community Redevelopment Agency

Table of Contents

Port Salerno 4

Executive Summary 6
    Salerno Road Sewer Enhancement
    Strategy

Project History 10
    Community Redevelopment Plan
    Zoning Overlays
    Vision to Reality

Utility Planning 14
    Utilities and Stormwater Master Plan
    Following the Plan
    Change in County Policy

Salerno Sewer Project 18
    NOW Visioning
    Outreach on Salerno Road
    Conceptual Design
    Community Support
    Economic Development Grants Tour
    Change in CRA Board

Final Design 22
    Community Support
    Focused Scope
    Maximizing the Return on Investment

Implementation 28
    Incremental Implementation
    Stormwater Retrofits
    Salerno Foot Bridge
    Commerce Avenue Demonstration Project

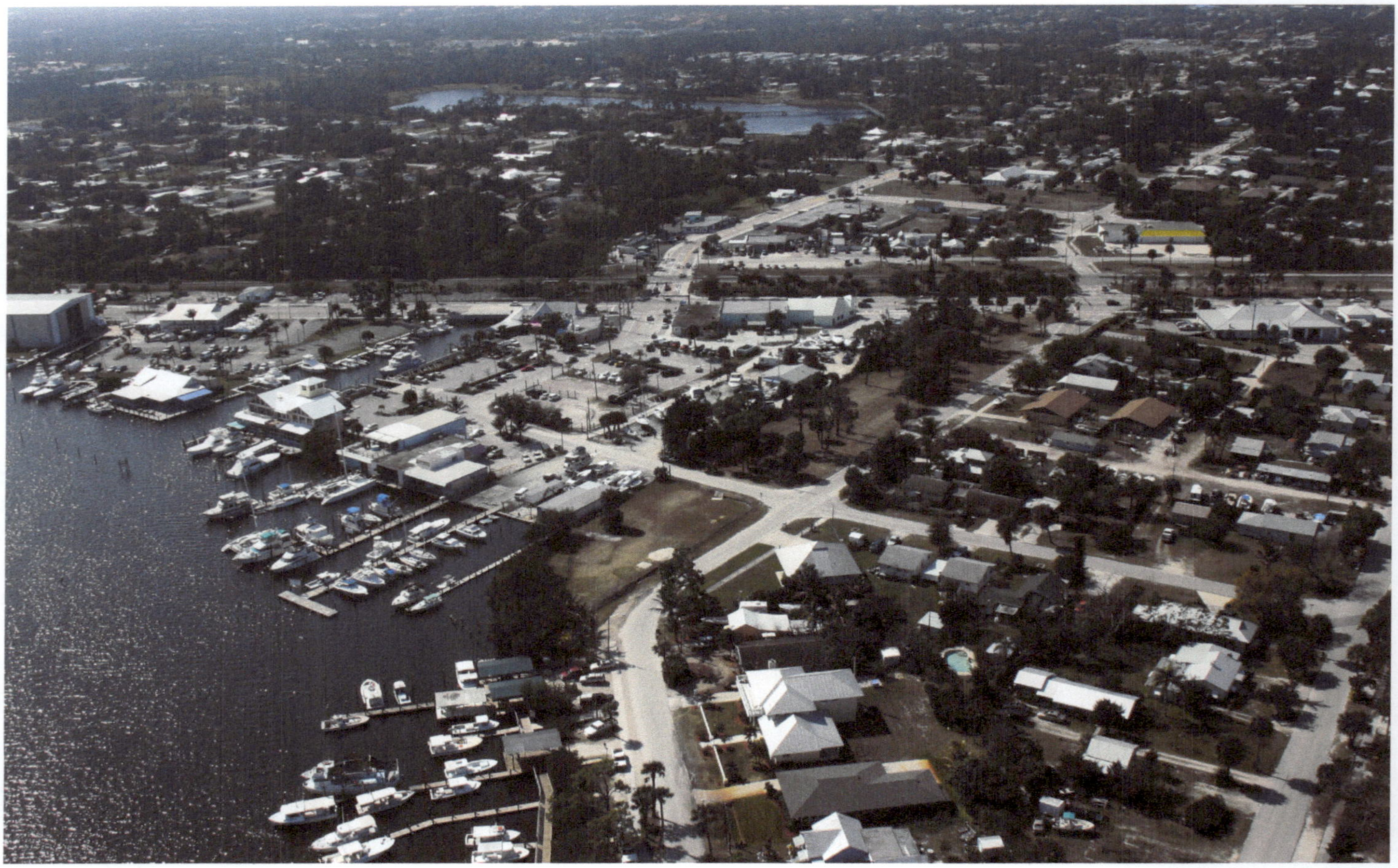

Area Summary

CRA Area: Port Salerno

Plan Adoption: May 2000

Total Area: 861 Acres

Area Highlights:

- Designated Florida waterfront community with residents and visitors enjoying the ever-increasing public waterfront access
- Economic base served largely by commercial and recreational fishing industry, in addition to boat manufacturing, repair and sales.

Special Designations:

- Waterfront Florida Community

Port Salerno

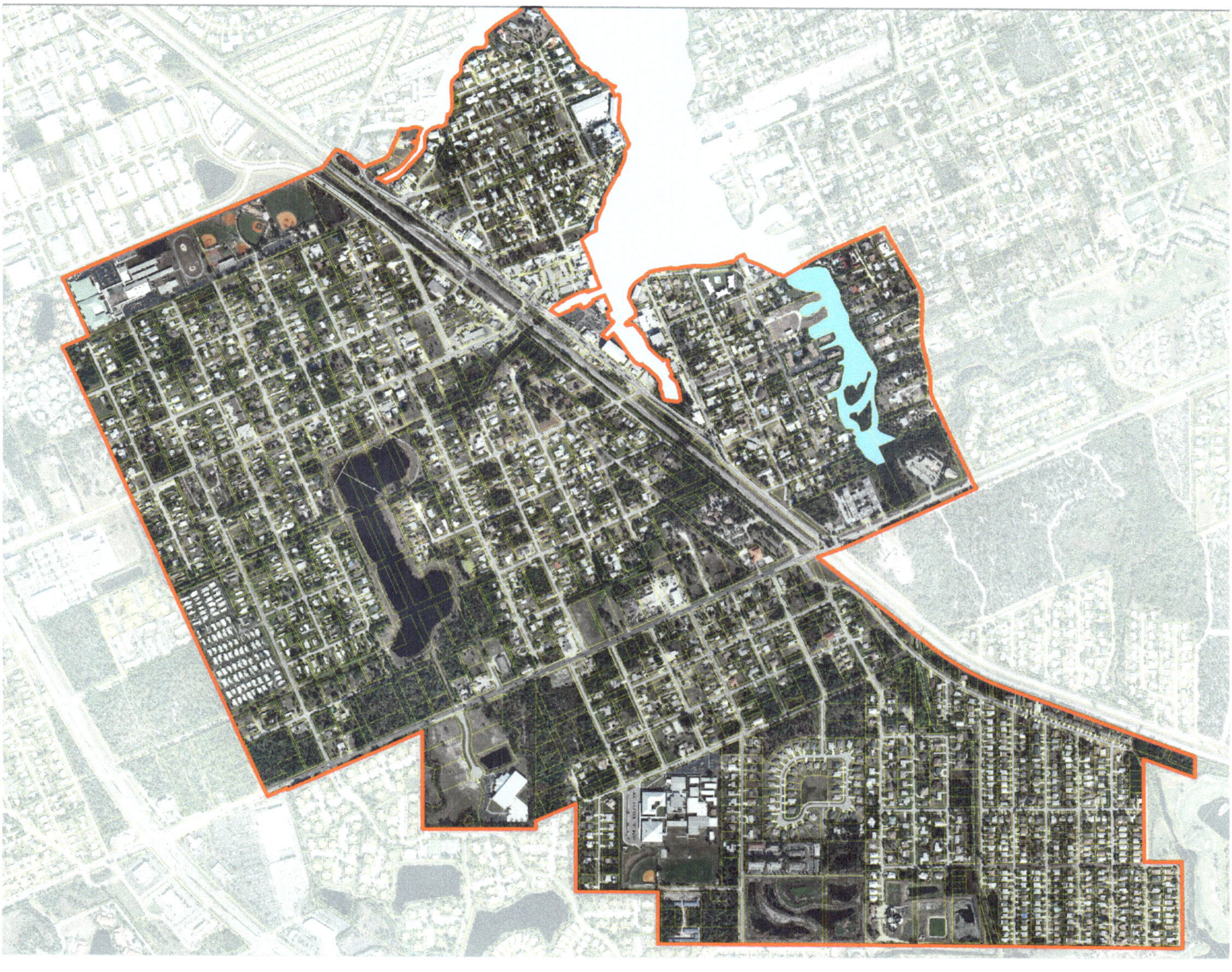

4

Salerno Road
Salerno Road
Commerce Avenue

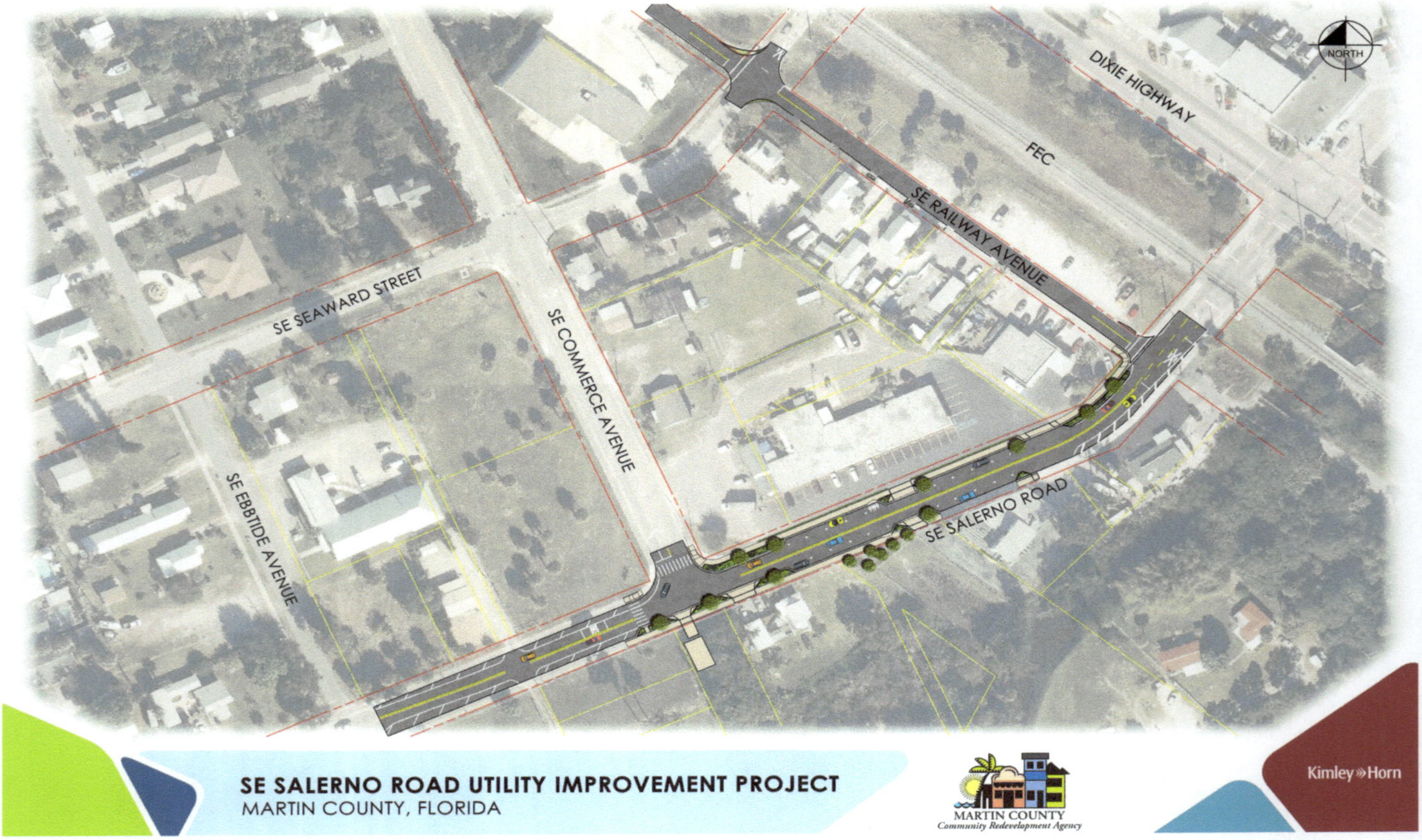
NORTH
DIXIE HIGHWAY
FEC
SE RAILWAY AVENUE
SE SEAWARD STREET
SE COMMERCE AVENUE
SE EBBTIDE AVENUE
SE SALERNO ROAD
SE SALERNO ROAD UTILITY IMPROVEMENT PROJECT
MARTIN COUNTY, FLORIDA
MARTIN COUNTY
Community Redevelopment Agency
Kimley»Horn

Above: *Concept drawings for the improvements for Salerno Road. Staff and the project engineering are refining these ideas with each adjacent property owner to maximize the benefit of this project.*

Executive Summary

Salerno Road Sewer Enhancement

Improvements to Salerno Road has been on the minds of residents since the inception of the Community Redevelopment Areas. This gateway into historic Port Salerno and the Manatee Pocket leads into the commercial and mixed-use core of the redevelopment area. Improvements on Dixie Highway and along the Pocket demonstrate the possibilities for private investment with the implementation of Complete Streets and expanded public utilities. This project achieves both without the need for additional right of way acquisition.

The Salerno Road Sewer Enhancement Project proposes a extension of the County's central sewer system on Salerno Road, from SE Commerce Avenue to Railway Avenue, and on Railway Avenue, from Salerno Road to 200 ft. north of Seaward St. which will enable existing businesses to utilize their full potential. The project will also introduce access management, on-street parking, pedestrian accommodations and low maintenance landscaping.

The benefits of the project go beyond the current scope, the lift station to be provided will enable additional sewer expansion into the residential neighborhoods to the west as funding becomes available in the future. The project includes a partnership with the Utilities Department.

Roadway improvements and utility design started on late June 2014 and is expected to be completed by early 2016, following season. The funding for this project is in place to complete this project.

Above: Salerno Road today and the project area.

7

Strategy

The Salerno Sewer enhancement project is just the first phase of a much larger utility project. This area of Salerno lacks public utilities, and the nearest forcemain is on the east side of the FEC rail tracks.

This project includes the extension of the forcemain under the FEC rail tracks, and includes a large lift station that will have the capacity to serve at least 17 blocks of residential and commercial properties. The Community Redevelopment Agency Capital Improvement Plan provides future funding to annually extend utilities throughout these established neighborhood.

The Community Redevelopment Agency (CRA) has successfully applied this strategy in the other redevelopment areas. In the Golden Gate Community

Redevelopment Area, the CRA was able to extend sewer off of Dixie Highway to the commercial properties on Bonita, Clayton, and Delmar Streets. The CRA has also commissioned plans to extend utilities to the remaining mixed-use and commercial properties as funding becomes available.

In the Rio Community Redevelopment Area, a Community Development Block Grant funded a similar size lift station off of Martin Avenue. This investment provided the infrastructure to extend utilities to all of the commercial properties along Dixie Highway in the Rio Town Center. This has also led to new redevelopment of Rio Porches and Rio Harbor. The CRA has also included expansion of utilities on an annual basis through the Capital Improvement Plan.

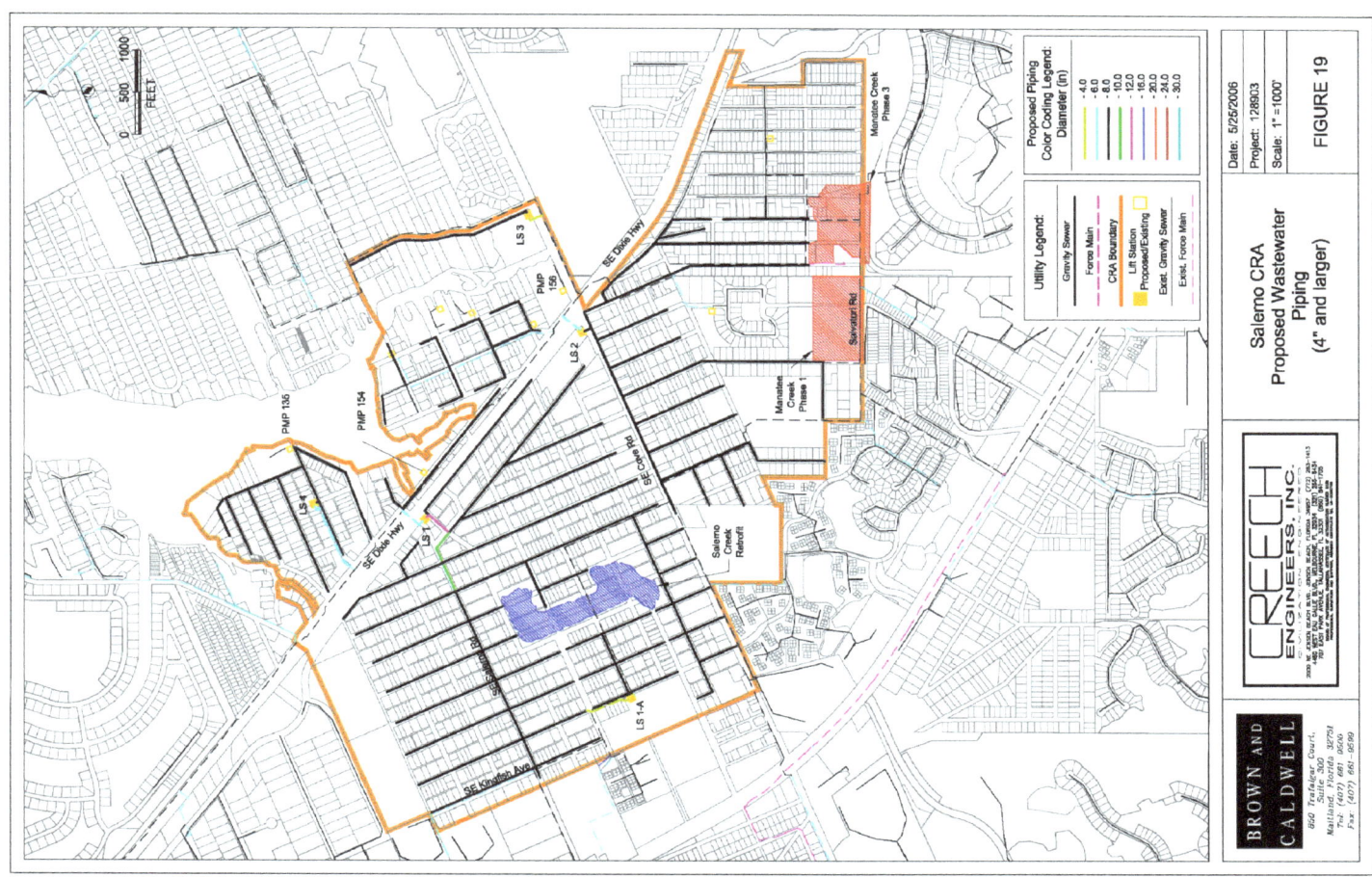

PORT SALERNO

Community Snapshot

VISION: "The '2020 Vision for a Sustainable Martin County' created the foundation for Port Salerno's vision of the future and its Community Redevelopment Plan with a focus on: Retention of Port Salerno's historic character and strengthening of neighborhoods, commercial centers, parks and the environment."

DESIGNATION: 2001

APPLICANT: Martin County

STATUS: Inactive; participates as a member of the Port Salerno CRA Neighborhood Advisory Committee.

KEY ACCOMPLISHMENTS: Established the Port Salerno Commercial Fishing Dock Authority; Initiated Phases 1-2 of Waterfront Boardwalk; Obtained funding for dredging at Manatee Pass; designed way-finding signs for downtown and the commercial pier.

CURRENT CHALLENGES: Assisting local businesses and homeowners with the dredging project; assisting the Port Salerno Commercial Fishing Dock Authority to design and build a more efficient and up-to-date dockside area for its operations.

FLORIDA ASSESSMENT OF COASTAL TRENDS DATA:

Number of Active Volunteers:	12
Volunteer Hours Contributed:	948
Public Dollars Contributed:	$9.3 million

Port Salerno
Community Redevelopment Plan
MARTIN COUNTY'S Historic Fishing Village

THE VISION

Conceptual Master Plan

New Post Office — 1

Salerno Creek Retrofit — 2
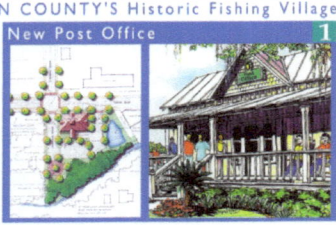

Cove/Salerno Roads Enhancement — 3

A1A Redesign and Enhancement — 7
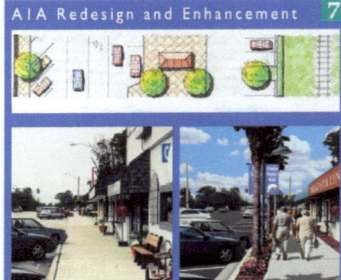

Port Salerno Civic Center Park — 6

Manatee Park/Commercial Docks — 5

Port Salerno Village Center Market Place — 4

Urban Design Principles

Preserve Port Salerno's Culture and History   Enhance and Connect Parks and Open Spaces   Establish a Livable Street Network

June 2000

Glatting Jackson Kercher Anglin Lopez Rinehart, Inc.

Project History

Community Redevelopment Plan

The planning process to enhance Salerno Road started prior the establishment of the Port Salerno Community Redevelopment. The residents of Port Salerno have been vocal advocates to protect the character of their community. Prior to the County's adoption of the county wide Community Redevelopment Agency in 1997, the residents of Port Salerno advocated for walkable, context sensitive street designs for the historic waterfront commercial district.

The Port Salerno Neighborhood Advisory Committee (NAC) identified Salerno Road as one of the top redevelopment focus area in 2000 in the adopted Port Salerno Community Redevelopment Plan. The plan identifies several projects that converge on Salerno Road.

- Establish a Master Stormwater and Utilities plan for Port Salerno
- Implement infrastructure improvements throughout the community
- Enhance and Connect Community Parks and Open Spaces
- Provide shaded sidewalks and bicycle lanes on Cove and Salerno Roads

Port Salerno
Community Redevelopment Plan

Prepared for:
The Martin County Community Redevelopment Agency
Port Salerno Neighborhood Advisory Committee

Prepared by:
Glatting Jackson Kercher Anglin Lopez Rinehart, Inc.
Williams, Hatfield & Stoner, Inc.

May 2000

Zoning Overlays

The Board of County Commissioners adopted the Port Salerno Zoning Overlay in August 2001 which supported the community vision through the Martin County Land Development Regulations. These regulations provided the opportunity for small scale infill and mixed-use development in Port Salerno. However, the lack of infrastructure made it difficult for the redevelopment of properties on Salerno Road.

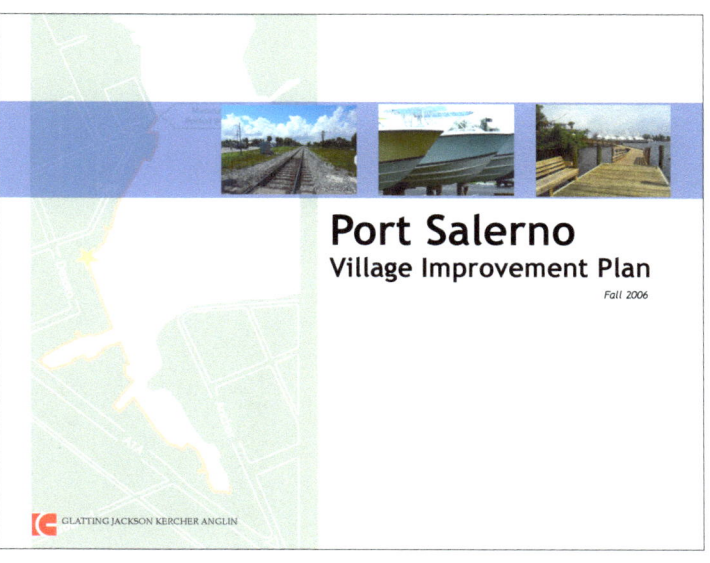

Port Salerno
Village Improvement Plan
Fall 2006

GLATTING JACKSON KERCHER ANGLIN

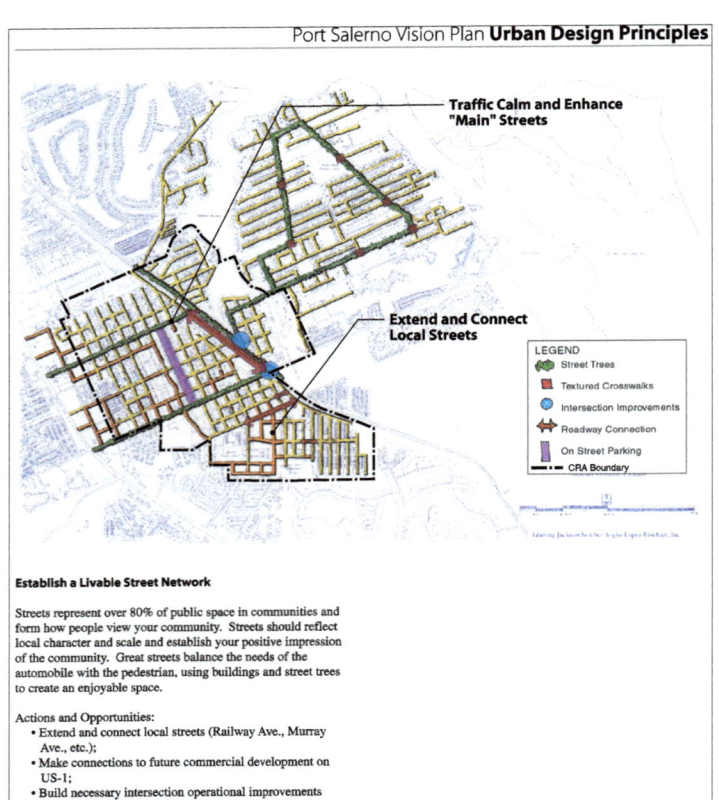

Traffic Calm and Enhance "Main" Streets

Extend and Connect Local Streets

LEGEND
- Street Trees
- Textured Crosswalks
- Intersection Improvements
- Roadway Connection
- On Street Parking
- CRA Boundary

Establish a Livable Street Network

Streets represent over 80% of public space in communities and form how people view your community. Streets should reflect local character and scale and establish your positive impression of the community. Great streets balance the needs of the automobile with the pedestrian, using buildings and street trees to create an enjoyable space.

Actions and Opportunities:
- Extend and connect local streets (Railway Ave., Murray Ave., etc.);
- Make connections to future commercial development on US-1;
- Build necessary intersection operational improvements (Railway/Cove Road intersection, A1A/Binnacle intersection);
- Relocate F.E.C. rail crossing from Broward St. to Market

Cove and Salerno Roads Enhancement

Cost: $2,000,000

Funding Sources: General Fund

Time-Frame:
A1A Intersections: 1-5 years
Roadway Enhancements: 5-10 years

Salerno and Cove Roads are east/west neighborhood collectors providing Port Salerno residents access to A1A and US-1. The proposed enhancement of Salerno and Cove Roads should include converting the roads to urban sections (enclosed drainage with curb and gutter), adding bicycle lanes, sidewalks, street trees and pedestrian level lighting. The reconstruction of the roads with curb and gutter will allow a regular planting of street trees closer to the road than currently allowed. The physical "enclosure" of the street with trees has the psychological effect of slowing down motorists.

Cove and Salerno Roads are important gateways to Port Salerno. The A1A intersections should receive special treatment, calm traffic, and provide an aesthetic and safe connection to the A1A business district and the waterfront.

Implementation
Funding for the design and construction of these improvements should be identified and scheduled in the County's Transportation Improvement Program (TIP).

Location Map

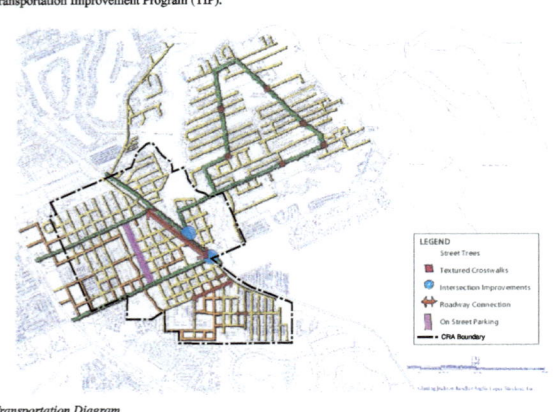

LEGEND
- Street Trees
- Textured Crosswalks
- Intersection Improvements
- Roadway Connection
- On Street Parking
- CRA Boundary

Transportation Diagram

Port Salerno
Post Office
Martin County, Florida

July 1999

Glatting Jackson Kercher Anglin Lopez Rinehart, Inc.

New Port Salerno Post Office Plan

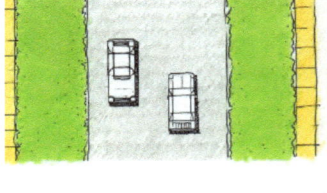

Existing Section of Cove / Salerno Roads   *Proposed Section of Cove / Salerno Roads*

Vision to Reality

In 2003, the hard work that forged the community vision began to become implemented with the improvements on Dixie Highway. This work created the roadway section we see today on Dixie Highway that includes sidewalks, landscaping, on street parking, and several innovative intersection designs. As a result of these improvements to the downtown, both public and private investment began along Dixie highway including the Civic Center, and a Community Development Block Grant for Economic Development that funded sewer expansion for existing development and the construction the Finz Waterfront Grill.

The enhancements of Dixie Highway and these new developments focused the attention of the Community Redevelopment Agency to the redevelopment and public access to the waterfront through the construction of the Pocket Walk. In 2006, the Community Redevelopment Agency through the recommendation of the Neighborhood Advisory Committee revised the Port Salerno Community Redevelopment Plan to adopt the Port Salerno Village Improvement Plan. The plan expanded the vision for public access to the water.

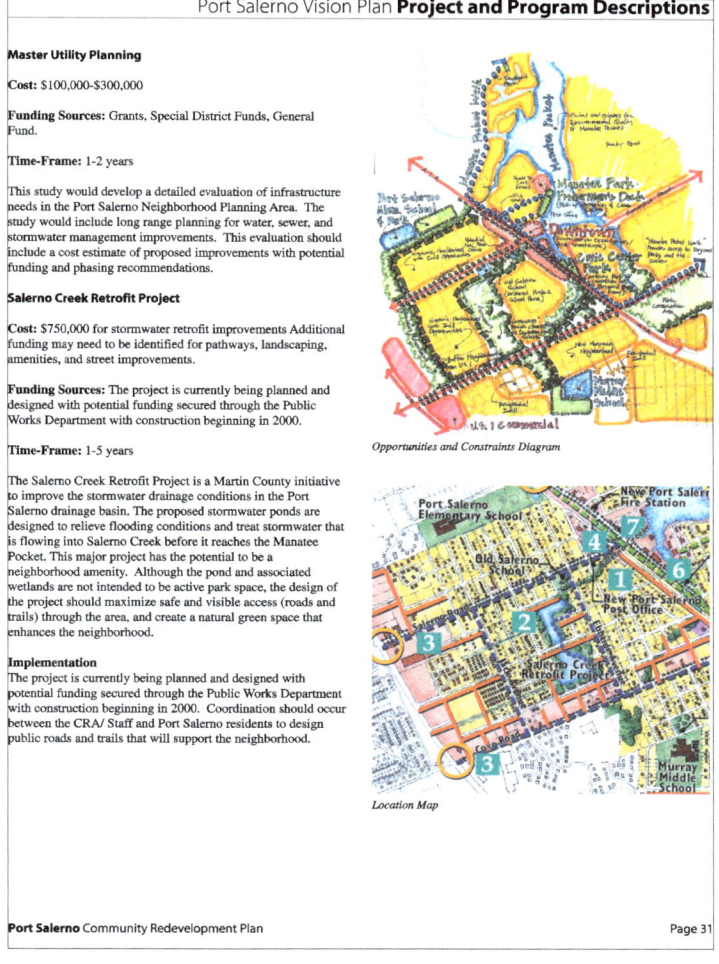

Master Utility Planning

Cost: $100,000-$300,000

Funding Sources: Grants, Special District Funds, General Fund.

Time-Frame: 1-2 years

This study would develop a detailed evaluation of infrastructure needs in the Port Salerno Neighborhood Planning Area. The study would include long range planning for water, sewer, and stormwater management improvements. This evaluation should include a cost estimate of proposed improvements with potential funding and phasing recommendations.

Salerno Creek Retrofit Project

Cost: $750,000 for stormwater retrofit improvements Additional funding may need to be identified for pathways, landscaping, amenities, and street improvements.

Funding Sources: The project is currently being planned and designed with potential funding secured through the Public Works Department with construction beginning in 2000.

Time-Frame: 1-5 years

The Salerno Creek Retrofit Project is a Martin County initiative to improve the stormwater drainage conditions in the Port Salerno drainage basin. The proposed stormwater ponds are designed to relieve flooding conditions and treat stormwater that is flowing into Salerno Creek before it reaches the Manatee Pocket. This major project has the potential to be a neighborhood amenity. Although the pond and associated wetlands are not intended to be active park space, the design of the project should maximize safe and visible access (roads and trails) through the area, and create a natural green space that enhances the neighborhood.

Implementation
The project is currently being planned and designed with potential funding secured through the Public Works Department with construction beginning in 2000. Coordination should occur between the CRA/ Staff and Port Salerno residents to design public roads and trails that will support the neighborhood.

Opportunities and Constraints Diagram

Location Map

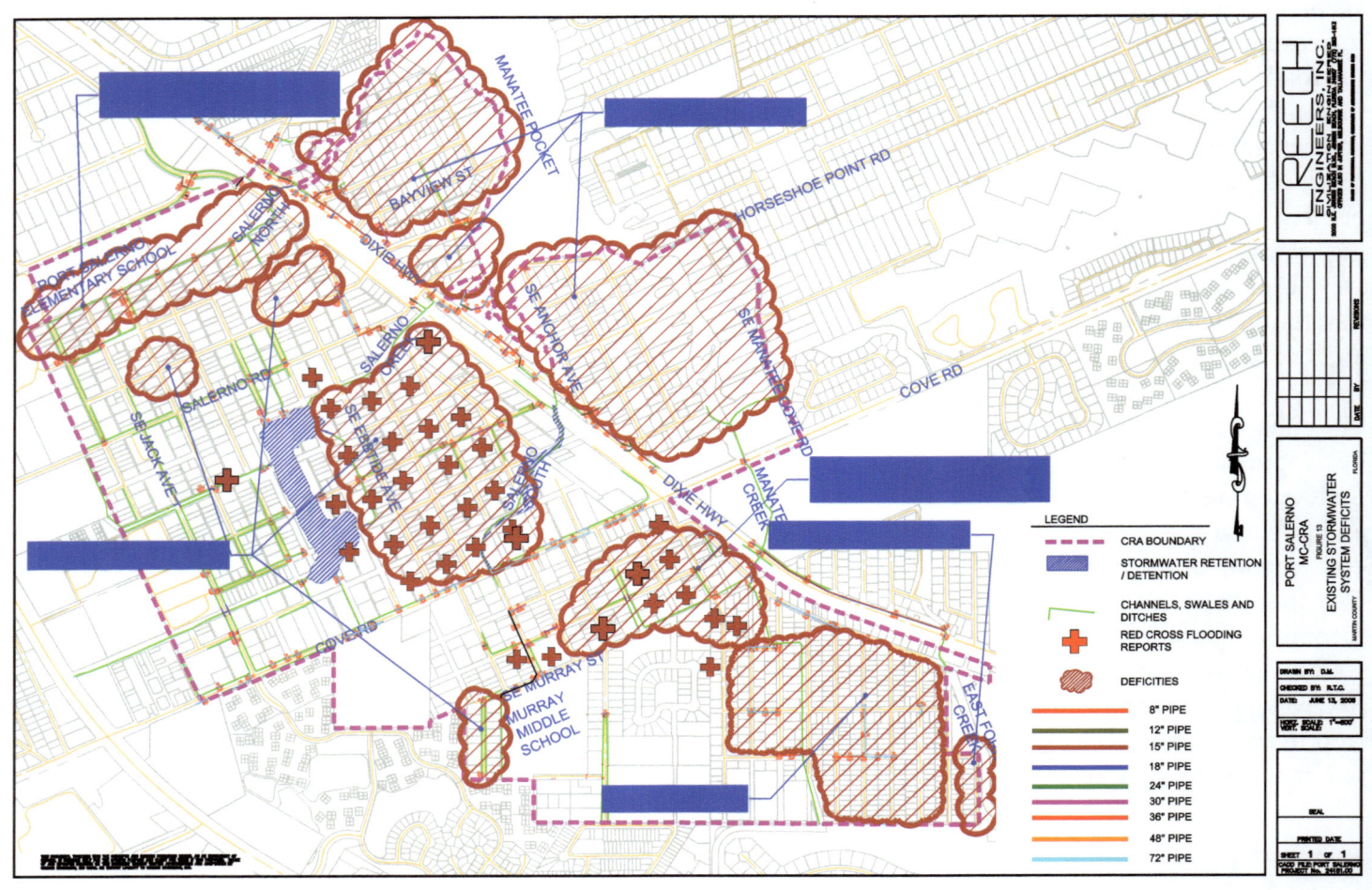

Opinion of Probable Cost Table

	Paving	Stormwater	Water	Wastewater	Streetscaping	Final Design	Permit Fees	Contingencies	Property Acquisition	Total
Dixie Park	$ 5,690,000	$ 4,010,000	$ 190,000	$ 440,000	$ 1,040,000	$ 1,240,000	$ 210,000	$ 3,100,000	$ -	$ 15,920,000
New Monrovia	$ 2,850,000	$ 2,970,000	$ 60,000	$ 670,000	$ 660,000	$ 790,000	$ 140,000	$ 1,970,000	$ 5,050,000	$ 15,160,000
Cove Road N	$ 5,660,000	$ 4,670,000	$ 880,000	$ 1,290,000	$ 1,250,000	$ 1,500,000	$ 250,000	$ 3,750,000	$ 3,950,000	$ 23,200,000
Salerno Road	$ 4,340,000	$ 3,950,000	$ 920,000	$ 940,000	$ 1,020,000	$ 1,220,000	$ 210,000	$ 3,050,000	$ 4,920,000	$ 20,570,000
Dixie Highway	$ 2,290,000	$ 1,760,000	$ 240,000	$ -	$ 430,000	$ 520,000	$ 90,000	$ 1,290,000	$ -	$ 6,620,000
Manatee Pocket S	$ 1,930,000	$ 2,160,000	$ 370,000	$ 630,000	$ 510,000	$ 620,000	$ 110,000	$ 1,530,000	$ 740,000	$ 8,600,000
Manatee Pocket N	$ 2,010,000	$ 2,830,000	$ 370,000	$ 570,000	$ 580,000	$ 700,000	$ 120,000	$ 1,740,000	$ 580,000	$ 9,500,000
Totals	$ 24,770,000	$ 22,350,000	$ 3,030,000	$ 4,540,000	$ 5,490,000	$ 6,590,000	$ 1,130,000	$ 16,430,000	$ 15,240,000	$ 99,570,000

Above: *Portions of the* Master Stormwater/Utility Plan illustrating the areas of need and Opinion of Probable Cost. This planning shows the magnitude of projects that need to be undertaken in Port Salerno.

Utility Planning

Utilities and Stormwater Master Plan

The Community Redevelopment Agency recognized that the lack of public utilities continued to be the biggest deterrent for redevelopment in Port Salerno.

In 2006, the Community Redevelopment Agency completed the Utilities and Stormwater Master Plan for Port Salerno which included a conceptual design and cost to complete all the necessary utilities and stormwater improvements for Port Salerno.

This Master Stormwater/Utility Plan provides guideline for construction and funding of infrastructure improvements necessary to meet the needs of Port Salerno in accordance with the Community Redevelopment Plan and the Neighborhood Advisory Committee's vision for the future of Port Salerno. The next step in this process is to use this Master Plan as a basis for construction and funding strategies that will take this from conceptual to reality.

The following steps are outlined in the Master Stormwater/Utility Plan to implement progress in the redevelopment area:

- **CONSTRUCTION PHASING:** A project of this magnitude typically is done in multiple phases which should be ranked in priority by the CRA.
- **FUNDING STRATEGY:** Explore all funding methodology (i.e., grants, loans, assessments, TIF funds) and set funding goals associated with the planned construction phasing.
- **PURSUIT OF GRANTS AND LOANS:** The CRA shall apply for all available grants and low interest loans in order to reduce the burden of costs for construction on the property owners within the CRA.
- **FINAL DESIGN:** Grant and loan applications require final design and construction drawings. Therefore, priority projects should move to final design.
- **CONSTRUCTION COORDINATION:** Prior to construction, Staff will coordinate an implementation plan to address scheduling, logistics, staging, communication, etc. with the property owners impacted by construction activities.
- **MASTER PLAN GATEKEEPER:** It is recommended that Martin County designate a "Project Gatekeeper" whose duties would include overseeing the Master Plan implementation.

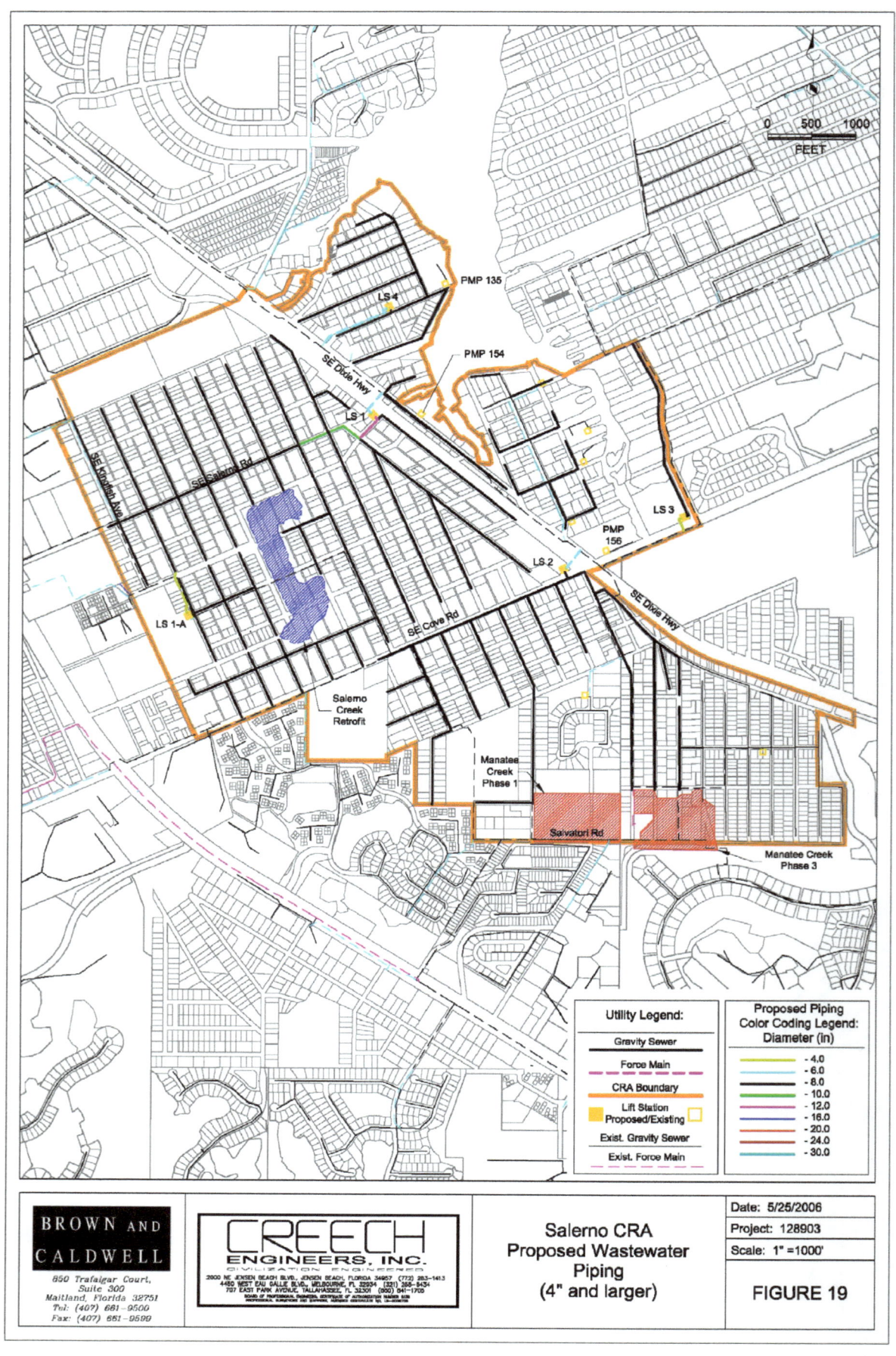

Utility Legend:

Gravity Sewer

Force Main

CRA Boundary

Lift Station
Proposed/Existing

Exist. Gravity Sewer

Exist. Force Main

Proposed Piping
Color Coding Legend:
Diameter (in)

- 4.0
- 6.0
- 8.0
- 10.0
- 12.0
- 16.0
- 20.0
- 24.0
- 30.0

BROWN AND CALDWELL
850 Trafalgar Court,
Suite 300
Maitland, Florida 32751
Tel: (407) 661-9500
Fax: (407) 661-9599

CREECH
ENGINEERS, INC.
CIVILIZATION ENGINEERED
2900 NE JENSEN BEACH BLVD., JENSEN BEACH, FLORIDA 34957 (772) 283-1413
4450 WEST EAU GALLIE BLVD., MELBOURNE, FL 32934 (321) 258-9434
707 EAST PARK AVENUE, TALLAHASSEE, FL 32301 (800) 541-1705
BOARD OF PROFESSIONAL ENGINEERS, CERTIFICATE OF AUTHORIZATION NUMBER 5230
PROFESSIONAL SURVEYORS AND MAPPERS, BUSINESS CERTIFICATE No. LB-0000709

Salerno CRA
Proposed Wastewater
Piping
(4" and larger)

Date: 5/25/2006

Project: 128903

Scale: 1"=1000'

FIGURE 19

PORT SALERNO COMMUNITY REDEVELOPMENT AREA
STORMWATER/UTILITY MASTER PLAN
MAXIMUM DEVELOPMENT POTENTIAL MATRIX
November 18, 2006 (Revised)

	AREA #	TOTAL AREA IN SQUARE FEET	TOTAL AREA IN ACRES	MAXIMUM PERCENT IMPERVIOUS AREA	TOTAL IMPERVIOUS AREA (SF)	TOTAL PERVIOUS AREA (SF)	MAXIMUM NUMBER OF UNITS PER ACRE	MAXIMUM TOTAL NUMBER OF UNITS FOR AREA	MAXIMUM PERCENT FLOOR AREA RATIO	MAXIMUM TOTAL FIRST FLOOR AREA (SF)
		GENERAL		STORM SEWER			WATER AND SANITARY SEWER			
CRA AREA NOT IN THE ZONING OR MIXED USE OVERLAY AREA										
PR - PUBLIC RECREATION						1,716,560		9		
PR	1	1,087,100	25.0	10	108,710	978,390	0.20	4.99		
	2	822,411	18.9	10	82,241	740,170	0.20	3.78		
RESIDENTIAL - ESTATE						723,629		66		
RES-ESTATE	1	1,447,258	33.2	50	723,629	723,629	2	66.45		
RESIDENTIAL - LOW						831,103		191		
RES-LOW	1	1,662,205	38.2	50	831,103	831,103	5	190.79		
RESIDENTIAL - MEDIUM						8,878,065		3261		
RES-MED	1	3,302,921	75.8	50	1,651,461	1,651,461	8	606.60		
	2	4,839,516	111.1	50	2,419,758	2,419,758	8	888.80		
	3	1,263,240	29.0	50	631,620	631,620	8	232.00		
	4	8,350,452	191.7	50	4,175,226	4,175,226	8	1533.60		
RESIDENTIAL - MOBILE HOME						1,333,771		490		
RES-MH	1	2,667,541	61.2	50	1,333,771	1,333,771	8	489.91		
GENERAL INDUSTRIAL						147,360		254		368,401
INDUST	1	736,802	16.9	80	589,442	147,360	15	253.72	50	368,401
GENERAL INSTITUTIONAL						91,755				229,387
INSTIT	1	458,774	10.5	80	367,019	91,755			50	229,387
GENERAL COMMERCIAL						3,485		6		10,454
CG	1	17,424	0.4	80	13,939	3,485	15	6.00	60	10,454
COMMERCIAL OFFICE RESIDENTIAL						252,840		218		252,840
COR	1	336,146	7.7	60	201,688	134,458	15	115.75	40	134,458
	2	295,953	6.8	60	177,572	118,381	15	101.91	40	118,381
COVE ROAD ZONING OVERLAY AREA										
MIXED USE OVERLAY / RESIDENTIAL - MEDIUM						321,338		369		
ZO/RES-MED	1	331,056	7.6	70	231,739	99,317	15	114.00		
	2	696,515	16.0	70	487,561	208,955	15	239.85		
	3	43,560	1.0	70	30,492	13,068	15	15.00		
MIXED USE OVERLAY / COMMERCIAL - GENERAL						35,318		41		70,635
ZO/CG	1	14,040	0.3	70	9,828	4,212	15	4.83	60	8,424
	2	17,424	0.4	70	12,197	5,227	15	6.00	60	10,454
	3	86,261	2.0	70	60,383	25,878	15	29.70	60	51,757
MIXED USE OVERLAY / COMMERCIAL - OFFICE - RESIDENTIAL						167,189		192		222,918
ZO/COR	1	557,296	12.8	70	390,107	167,189	15	191.91	40	222,918
GENERAL INDUSTRIAL						28,591		33		47,652
ZO/INDUST	1	95,303	2.2	70	66,712	28,591	15	32.82	50	47,652
MIXED USE OVERLAY AREA										
MIXED USE OVERLAY / RESIDENTIAL - LOW						270,072		372		
MUO/RES-LOW	1	1,080,288	24.8	75	810,216	270,072	15	372.00		
MIXED USE OVERLAY / RESIDENTIAL - MEDIUM						280,543		386		
MUO/RES-MED	1	609,672	14.0	75	457,254	152,418	15	209.94		
	2	111,509	2.6	75	83,632	27,877	15	38.40		
	3	89,893	2.1	75	67,420	22,473	15	30.95		
	4	202,437	4.6	75	151,828	50,609	15	69.71		
	5	94,130	2.2	75	70,598	23,533	15	32.41		
	6	14,531	0.3	75	10,898	3,633	15	5.00		
MIXED USE OVERLAY / RESIDENTIAL - MOBILE HOME						95,072		117		
MUO/RES-MH	1	340,287	7.8	75	255,215	85,072	15	117.18		
MIXED USE OVERLAY / COMMERCIAL - GENERAL						218,861		377		656,582
MUO/CG	1	814,572	18.7	80	651,658	162,914	15	280.50	60	488,743
	2	240,554	5.5	80	192,443	48,111	15	82.84	60	144,332
	3	12,042	0.3	80	9,634	2,408	15	4.15	60	7,225
	4	27,136	0.6	80	21,709	5,427	15	9.34	60	16,282
MIXED USE OVERLAY / COMMERCIAL - LIMITED						39,872		45		64,787
MUO/CL	1	28,856	0.7	70	20,199	8,657	15	9.94	50	14,428
	2	100,718	2.3	70	70,503	30,215	15	34.68	50	50,359
MIXED USE OVERLAY / COMMERCIAL - OFFICE - RESIDENTIAL						22,727		20		22,727
MUO/COR	1	37,030	0.9	60	22,218	14,812	15	12.75	40	14,812
	2	19,788	0.5	60	11,873	7,915	15	6.81	40	7,915
MIXED USE OVERLAY / COMMERCIAL - WATERFRONT						286,574		295		427,623
MUO/CW	1	805,860	18.5	70	564,102	241,758	15	277.50	50	402,930
	2	27,606	0.6	70	19,324	8,282	15	9.51	50	13,803
	3	21,780	0.5	70	15,246	6,534	15	7.50	50	10,890
MIXED USE OVERLAY / GENERAL INSTITUTIONAL						54,487		94		136,217
MUO/INSTIT	1	99,752	2.3	80	79,802	19,950	15	34.35	50	49,876
	2	172,682	4.0	80	138,146	34,536	15	59.46	50	86,341
TOWN CENTER MIXED USE OVERLAY AREA										
RESIDENTIAL LOW						317,988		219		
TC/RES-LOW	1	635,976	14.6	50	317,988	317,988	15	219.00		
RESIDENTIAL - MOBILE HOME						224,334		155		
TC/RES-MED	1	47,916	1.1	50	23,958	23,958	15	16.50		
	2	400,752	9.2	50	200,376	200,376	15	138.00		
RESIDENTIAL - HIGH						45,738		21		
TC/RES-HIGH	1	91,476	2.1	50	45,738	45,738	10	21.00		
COMMERCIAL - OFFICE - RESIDENTIAL						20,201		17		20,201
TC/COR	1	50,502	1.2	60	30,301	20,201	15	17.39	40	20,201
COMMERCIAL - WATERFRONT						89,227		68		148,711
TC/CW	1	243,293	5.6	70	170,305	72,988	10	55.85	50	121,647
	2	54,129	1.2	70	37,890	16,239	10	12.43	50	27,065

Left: The Master Utility Plan show the areas of need as of 2006. Some of these projects have been completed.
Above: The Plan is based on the development potential as allocated in Martin County Comprehensive Growth Management Plan Future Land Use Map.

Following the Plan

In accordance to the Master Stormwater/Utility Plan, the Community Redevelopment Agency worked with the Neighborhood Advisory Committee (NAC) to prioritize the projects in the plan. This planning took place during the NAC with input from a broad base of community stakeholders.

In 2007, Port Salerno Neighborhood Advisory Committee prioritized Capital Improvement Projects. The consensus was to prioritize as follows:
- Manatee Pocket dredging
- Stormwater management focusing on areas prioritized by the Stormwater Management Department
- Salerno Road Sewer and Water

In March, 2008, Port Salerno Neighborhood Advisory Committee recommended that the Community Redevelopment Agency (Board of County Commissioners) to proceed with the bidding process for the engineering design of sewer at Salerno Road from Jack to Dixie. Estimated design cost was $315,000. Estimated construction cost was $2,000,000, and at that time, no funds were available for the construction of such a project.

In 2008, staff coordinated with the Utilities Department to develop a scope of services to design a sewer system for Salerno, and CRA Staff explored the possibility of bonding capital projects such as this.

Change in County Policy

In 2009, due to the declines in property values and reductions in tax Revenue County wide, the County Administrator instituted a new county wide policy prohibiting the design of any County Capital Improvement Projects, unless construction funding was allocated. This placed the design of this project on hold.

PORT SALERNO
COMMUNITY REDEVELOPMENT AREA

Martin County CRA

Port Salerno 6

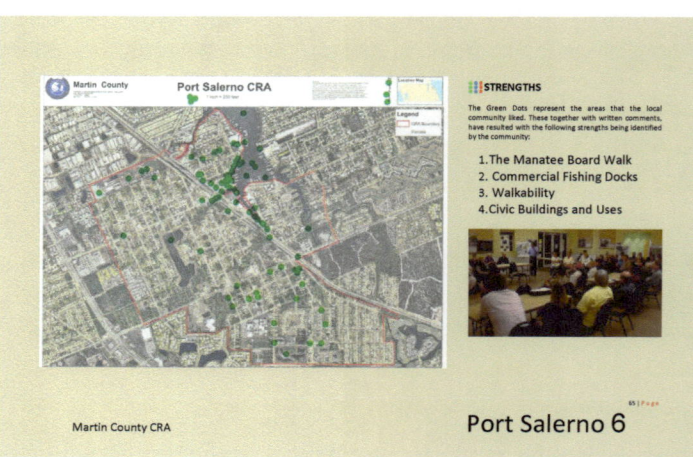

STRENGTHS

The Green Dots represent the areas that the local community liked. These together with written comments, have resulted with the following strengths being identified by the community:

1. The Manatee Board Walk
2. Commercial Fishing Docks
3. Walkability
4. Civic Buildings and Uses

Martin County CRA

Port Salerno 6

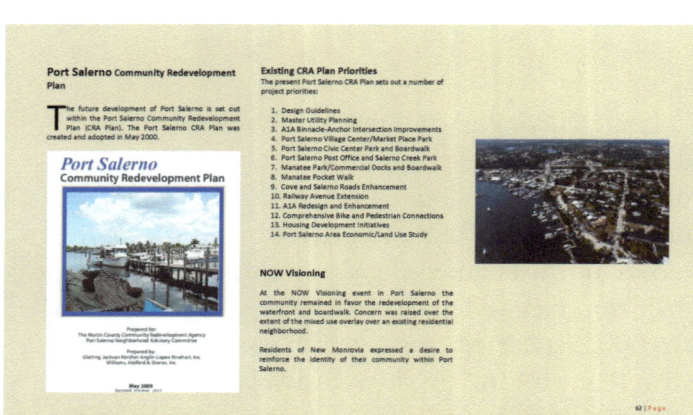

Port Salerno Community Redevelopment Plan

The future development of Port Salerno is set out within the Port Salerno Community Redevelopment Plan (CRA Plan). The Port Salerno CRA Plan was created and adopted in May 2000.

Existing CRA Plan Priorities

The present Port Salerno CRA Plan sets out a number of project priorities:

1. Design Guidelines
2. Master Utility Planning
3. A1A Binnacle-Anchor Intersection improvements
4. Port Salerno Village Center/Market Place Park
5. Port Salerno Civic Center Park and Boardwalk
6. Port Salerno Post Office and Salerno Creek Park
7. Manatee Park/Commercial Docks and Boardwalk
8. Manatee Pocket Walk
9. Cove and Salerno Roads Enhancement
10. Railway Avenue Extension
11. A1A Redesign and Enhancement
12. Comprehensive Bike and Pedestrian Connections
13. Housing Development Initiatives
14. Port Salerno Area Economic/Land Use Study

NOW Visioning

At the NOW Visioning event in Port Salerno the community remained in favor the redevelopment of the waterfront and boardwalk. Concern was raised over the extent of the mixed use overlay over an existing residential neighborhood.

Residents of New Monrovia expressed a desire to reinforce the identity of their community within Port Salerno.

Martin County CRA

Port Salerno 6

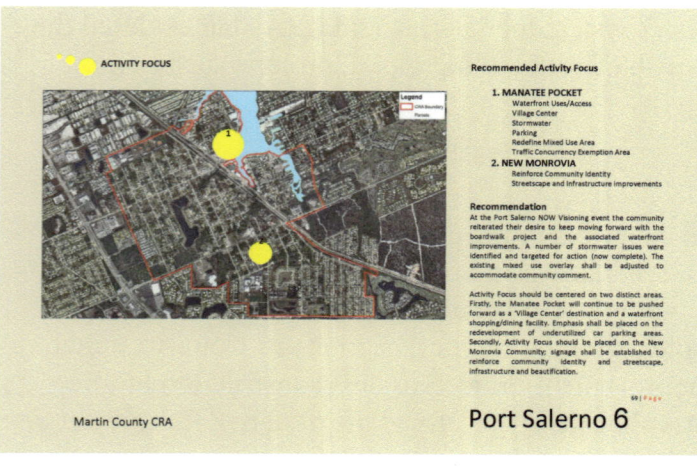

ACTIVITY FOCUS

Recommended Activity Focus

1. **MANATEE POCKET**
   Waterfront Uses/Access
   Village Center
   Stormwater
   Parking
   Redefine Mixed Use Area
   Traffic Concurrency Exemption Area

2. **NEW MONROVIA**
   Reinforce Community Identity
   Streetscape and Infrastructure improvements

Recommendation

At the Port Salerno NOW Visioning event the community reiterated their desire to keep moving forward with the boardwalk project and the associated waterfront improvements. A number of stormwater issues were identified and targeted for action (now complete). The existing mixed use overlay shall be adjusted to accommodate community comment.

Activity Focus should be centered on two distinct areas. Firstly, the Manatee Pocket will continue to be pushed forward as a 'Village Center' destination and a waterfront shopping/dining facility. Emphasis shall be placed on the redevelopment of underutilized car parking areas. Secondly, Activity Focus should be placed on the New Monrovia Community; signage shall be established to reinforce community identity and streetscape, infrastructure and beautification.

Martin County CRA

Port Salerno 6

Salerno Sewer Project

NOW Visioning

In 2009, the Community Development Department hired a new Director, Kev Freeman. He began a series called the Neighborhood Opportunities Workshop (NOW) Visioning. These two day public workshops provided the residents, property owners, and business owners of the community redevelopment area a venue to share the strengths, weaknesses and opportunities of their community. This public input built consensus on the Recommended Activity Focus areas. In the case of Port Salerno the Recommended Activity Focus was on enhancing the Village Center of the Manatee Pocket which included the need for infrastructure improvements including parking, stormwater, and the Expansion of Water and Sewer.

In 2010, downtown Port Salerno began to improve faster than other commercial areas in central Martin County. The Now Visioning target focus areas and the success of the Pocket Walk led to renewed commercial development interest the Community Redevelopment Agency to focus on Salerno Road.

Outreach on Salerno Road

Community Development Staff began meeting with property and business owners along Salerno Road to discuss possible improvements to this area, specifically the benefits of expanding sewer on Salerno Road. Local businesses explained the need for public utilities, the vision for a safer street, and the desire for more parking.

Conceptual Design

In April, 2011, the Community Redevelopment Agency contracted with Martin County Utilities to prepare design and construction plans for the phase one Utility improvements on Salerno Road from Commerce Ave. to Railway Ave.; and on Railway Ave. from Salerno Road to Seaward. These plans were developed to obtain a more realistic design and probable cost for utility expansion on Salerno Road, and identified that much of the roadway would need to be repaved with this utility expansion. This scope cost the CRA under $25,000.

Initial designs demonstrated that a smaller first phase of sewer could be constructed within an achievable budget; staff began to explore how Salerno road could be reconfigured with the required repaving to achieve the community vision adopted in the Community Redevelopment Plan. This project also provided the opportunity to reconfigure the utilization of the right of way, so that the finished project would follow the community vision adopted in the redevelopment plan.

In May, 2011, a Consultant with experience in complete streets and roadway retrofits on existing commercial corridors (Kimley-Horn and Associates Inc.) was hired to provide urban corridor planning at for Salerno Road from SE Ebbtide Avenue to SE Railway Avenue, approximately 1,000 linear feet; SE Commerce Avenue from SE Salerno Road to SE Seaward Street, approximately 500 linear feet; and, SE Railway Avenue from SE Salerno Road to SE Seaward Street, approximately 550 linear feet. The purpose of this preliminary design is to evaluate the reconstruction of the streets within the context of "complete streets". The complete streets approach evaluates the needs and accommodations of the motorist, pedestrian, bicyclist, transit user and corridor user alike. The cost of this preliminary roadway design work was $23,250.

Preliminary analysis showed that these surface level improvements could provide significant improvements to the corridor in accordance with the community vision, with little impact to the project budget. In order to begin the next step in the design, in May, 2011, Northstar Geomatics Inc was hired to provide professional surveying/mapping services for the utilities and roadway design of the project. The cost of this surveying work was $29,700.

In August of 2011, Staff reviewed the 90% design plans for proposed gravity sewer on Salerno Road, and the roadway concept plans for consistency with the community redevelopment plan. In September, 2011, Kimley Horn and Associates Inc. presented an overview of the roadway concept plans developed for the Salerno Road Corridor Plan to the Port Salerno NAC members. A project pamphlet was created to highlight the project scope and possible transformation of Salerno Road into a street similar to Dixie Highway. Business and property owners along Salerno Road attended the meeting to share their excitement and support of the project.

Community Support

With the support of the Neighborhood Advisory Committee (NAC), and the support of the local property and business owners, Staff presented this project to the Community Redevelopment Agency. The Agency supported the continued survey and design work to complete this project. Staff also worked to seek various funding sources based on the initial probable cost for construction.

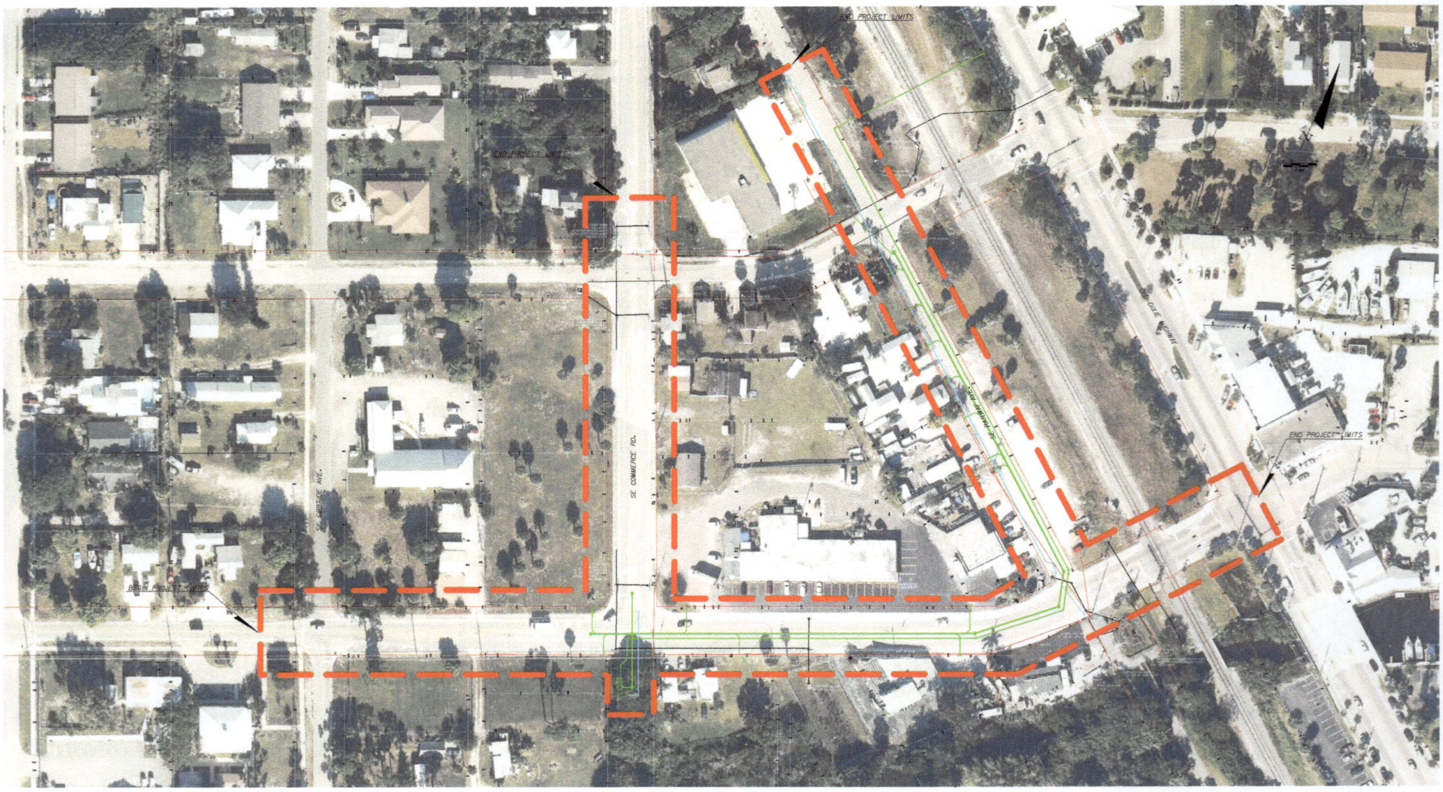

September, 2012, Staff received several communications from community members and business owners along Salerno Road requesting updates on the availability of funds for the project. They reiterated how important the project is for the corridor. With the uncertainty of TIF funding from the Board of County Commissioners, CDD Staff worked with the Utilities Department to get an estimate of the assessment cost for each property to fund the project construction. The rate of assessment for each ERC exceeded the allowable ratio of assessment cost to property value, making the assessment a non-feasible option to fund the project. The project would require public investment to be feasible.

Economic Development Grants Tour

In 2012 the Governor of Florida created a new Office of Economic opportunity which focused on providing grant funds to local governments and low interest loans to small businesses in return for job creation. The Community Development Department hosted a workshop in Martin County for local businesses to meet with the Office of Economic Opportunity, and toured these representatives throughout Martin County including Port Salerno. The competitiveness for these funds across the state and the complexity of the program requirements for these funds made it cumbersome for small businesses to participate. Also due to the budget conscience scope of the project, staff wasn't able to get enough jobs match to get a sizeable enough Economic Development grant to offset the cost of installing the project.

Change in CRA Board

In December 2012 the Board of County Commissioners adopted the ordinance amending Chapter 39, General Ordinances of the Martin County Code, by changing the members of the Martin County Community Redevelopment Agency to members of the Board of County Commissioners. A restructuring of the NAC's was also part of this

ordinance which generated the suspension of all Neighborhood Advisory Committee meetings until appropriate action is taken by the Board of County Commissioners.

At the Board of County Commissioner's direction, staff paused work on all Capital Projects, and focused on the restructuring of the Community Redevelopment Agency and the Neighborhood Advisory Committees. The 2012 and 2013 annual report reflects the completion of construction projects, and new private investment in Port Salerno. It was not until September, 2013 until the new Neighborhood Advisory Committee members were appointed for each redevelopment area.

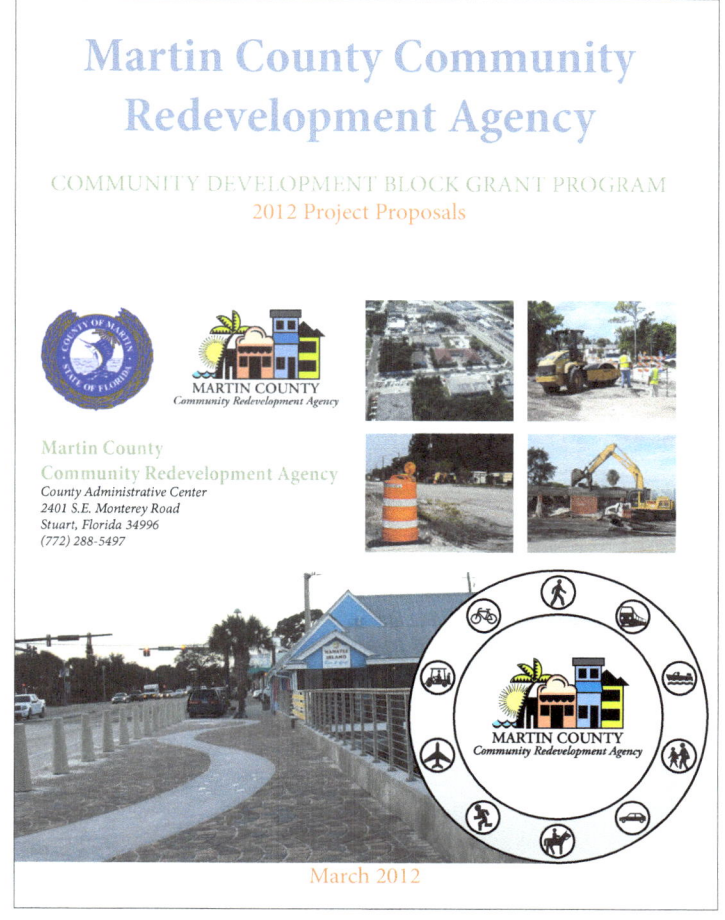

20

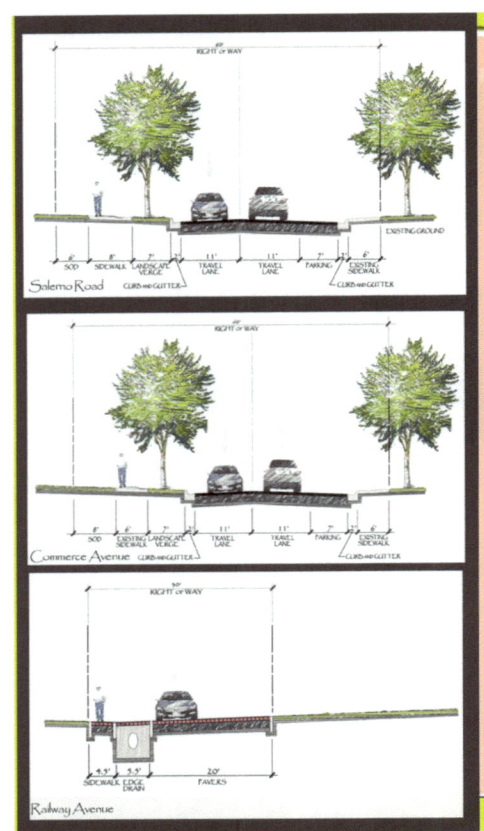

RIGHT of WAY
EXISTING GROUND
6' SOD
8' SIDEWALK
7' LANDSCAPE VERGE
2'
11' TRAVEL LANE
11' TRAVEL LANE
7' PARKING
2'
6' EXISTING SIDEWALK
CURB AND GUTTER
CURB AND GUTTER
Salerno Road
RIGHT of WAY
8' SOD
6' EXISTING SIDEWALK
7' LANDSCAPE VERGE
2'
11' TRAVEL LANE
11' TRAVEL LANE
7' PARKING
2'
6' EXISTING SIDEWALK
CURB AND GUTTER
CURB AND GUTTER
Commerce Avenue
50' RIGHT of WAY
4.5' SIDEWALK
5.5' EDGE DRAIN
20' PAVERS
Railway Avenue

SE Bayview St
SE Park Dr
Georges Way
Commerce Ave
SE Flobide Ave
SE Seaward St
Salerno Road
Project Limits
SE Railway Ave
SE Driftwood Ave
SE Channel Dr
SE Broward St
Project Location Map
Not to Scale
Kimley-Horn and Associates, Inc.
salerno road
Corridor Improvements
MARTIN COUNTY
Community Redevelopment Agency

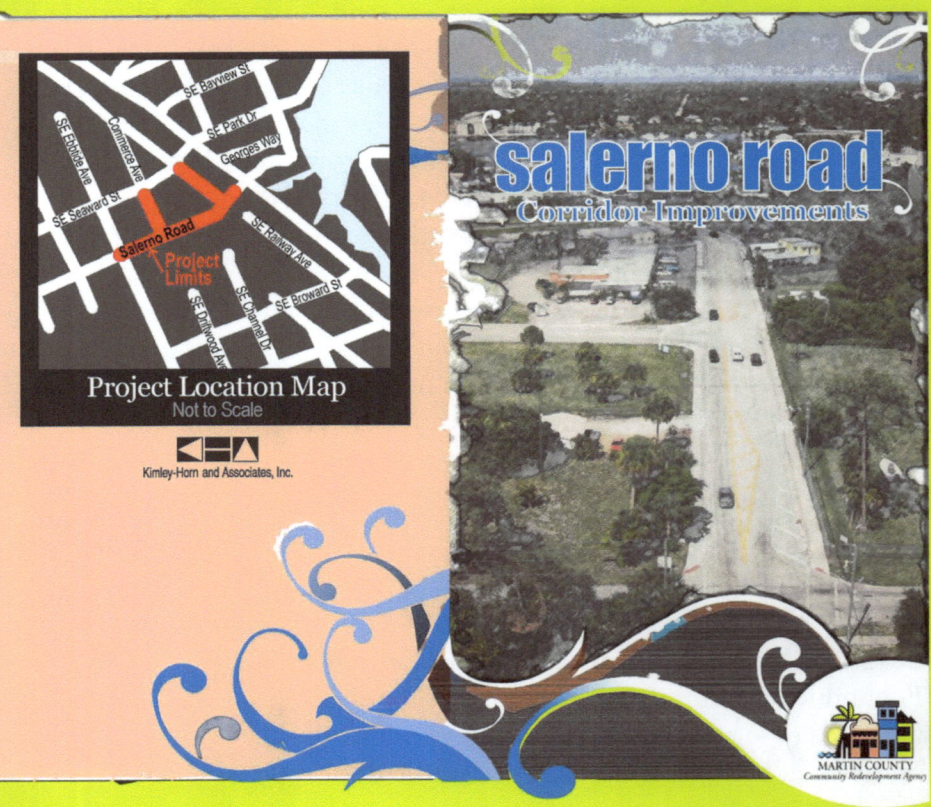

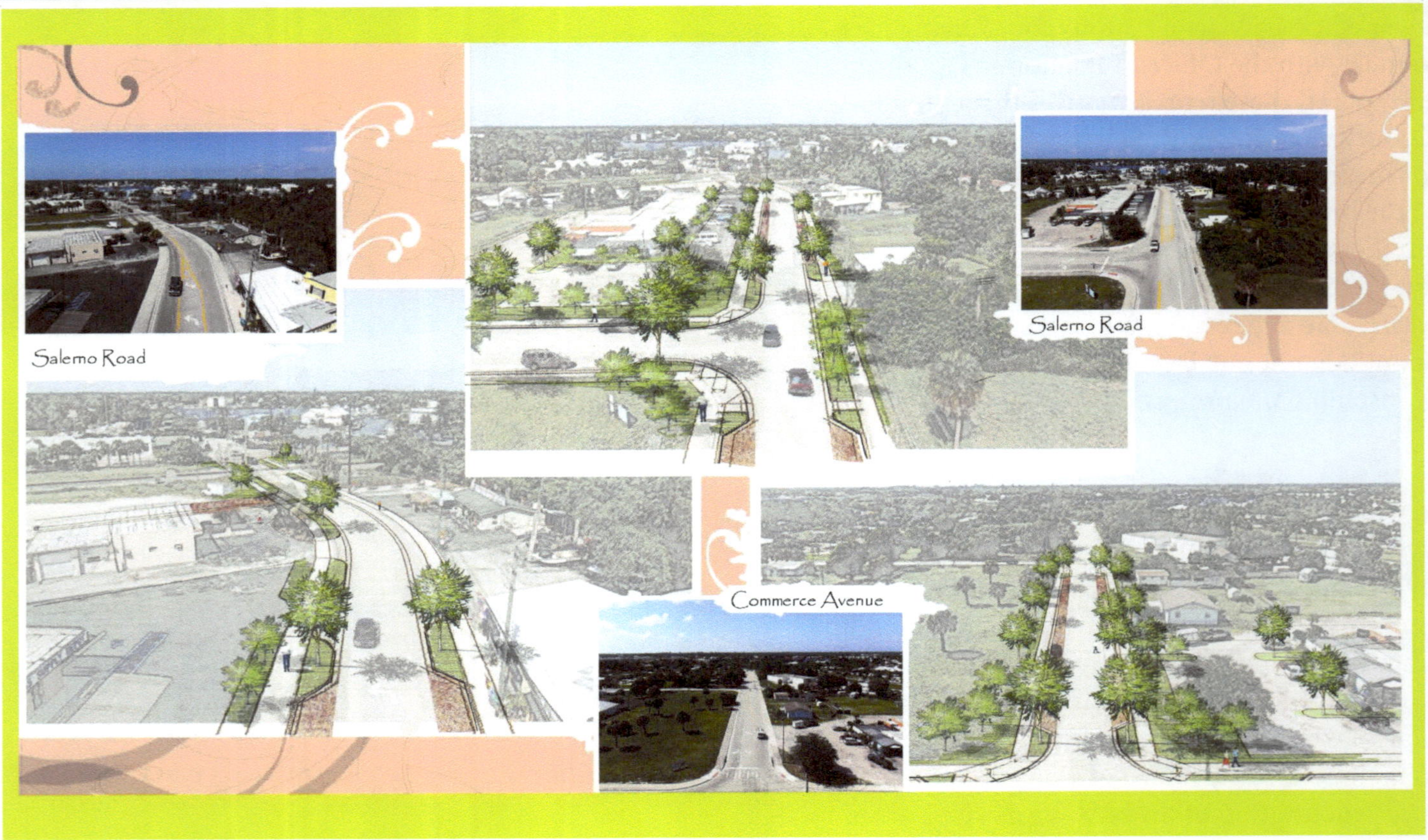

Salerno Road
Salerno Road
Commerce Avenue

Final Design

Community Support

When the new Neighborhood Advisory Committee met in September 2013, residents, business owners, and the NAC shared their continued desire to extend utilities on Salerno Road. In November 2013, with no availability of grant funds, Community Development Department staff proposed a partnership with the Utilities Department to gather funding to make possible to move forward with the Salerno Sewer Project. The Utilities Department agreed to partner with the CRA and offered to allocate $225,000 to assist with the cost of the lift station needed to extend gravity sewer along Salerno Road. This introduction of funds opened up a new opportunity for the project to become a reality and a new budget for the project was established using the allocations from MCU and CRA.

Focused Scope

In February 2014, a new project scope was created based on the available funds. The new scope would reduce the extension of the roadway improvements to allow for a complete design and construction. The Scope of work included: SE Salerno Rd – from SE Commerce Ave. to Railway Ave. approx. 600 linear feet; SE Railway Ave. – from 200-ft north of SE Seaward St. to SE Salerno Rd. approx. 680 linear feet; and, Florida East Coast Railway – between SE Railway Ave. to SE Dixie Hwy. approx. 240 linear feet.

This first phase of the sewer project would complete the most critical first step in extending water and sewer west of Dixie Highway. The project is being designed with a lift station with the capacity to serve properties along Salerno Road west to Grouper Avenue. This would allow for expansion of the system, as funding permitted.

In March 2014 the new project scope for the Salerno Road Sewer Enhancement Project was presented to the NAC and community members for their review. NAC members expressed their support for the project and encouraged staff to move forward with its design and construction.

A scope of work for 100% design plans with the new project scope was prepared in April 2014. The scope of work included the completion of the previously developed 90% utility plans, and the development of 30%, 60% and final design plans for the roadway sections. The scope of work included a provision for the consultant to develop a project consistent with the available funding. The Design costs included the following tasks:

- Geotechnical Investigation
- Roadway Analysis and Plans
- Drainage Plans
- Utility Analysis and Plans
- Agency Permitting
- Signing and Pavement Marking Plans
- Public Involvement / Coordination

The total cost of the complete project design is $116,235.

A Notice to proceed with the project design was given to the selected Engineering consultant, Kimley-Horn and Associates, Inc. was issued June 2014.

September 2014 – 30% Roadway Design Plans were submitted by the engineering consultant. The submitted plans are to be reviewed by several County departments including Community Development, Engineering, Utilities and, Information and technology.

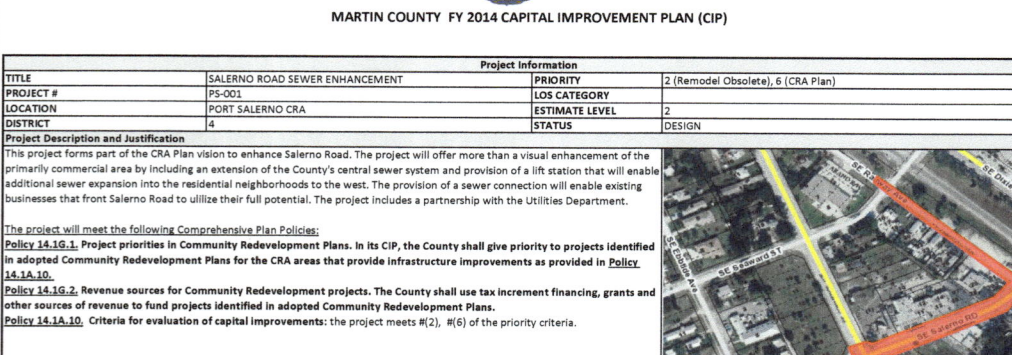

Top: *The Master Utility Plan update showing the possible sewer expansion with the construction of the lift station on Salerno Road.*

Left: *The FY 2014 Capital Improvement Sheet showing the scope and budget proposed for this first phase of sewer expansion west of Dixie Highway.*

MARTIN COUNTY FY 2014 CAPITAL IMPROVEMENT PLAN (CIP)

Project Information			
TITLE	SALERNO ROAD SEWER ENHANCEMENT	PRIORITY	2 (Remodel Obsolete), 6 (CRA Plan)
PROJECT #	PS-001	LOS CATEGORY	
LOCATION	PORT SALERNO CRA	ESTIMATE LEVEL	2
DISTRICT	4	STATUS	DESIGN

Project Description and Justification

This project forms part of the CRA Plan vision to enhance Salerno Road. The project will offer more than a visual enhancement of the primarily commercial area by including an extension of the County's central sewer system and provision of a lift station that will enable additional sewer expansion into the residential neighborhoods to the west. The provision of a sewer connection will enable existing businesses that front Salerno Road to utilize their full potential. The project includes a partnership with the Utilities Department.

The project will meet the following Comprehensive Plan Policies:

Policy 14.1G.1. Project priorities in Community Redevelopment Plans. In its CIP, the County shall give priority to projects identified in adopted Community Redevelopment Plans for the CRA areas that provide infrastructure improvements as provided in Policy 14.1A.10.

Policy 14.1G.2. Revenue sources for Community Redevelopment projects. The County shall use tax increment financing, grants and other sources of revenue to fund projects identified in adopted Community Redevelopment Plans.

Policy 14.1A.10. Criteria for evaluation of capital improvements: the project meets #(2), #(6) of the priority criteria.

Operating Budget Impact

Expenditures	Total	To Date		FY14	FY15	FY16	FY17	FY18	FY19	FY20	FY21	FY22	FY23
Design	150,000	30,000		120,000									
Construction	2,375,000				1,575,000	200,000	200,000	200,000	200,000				
Land	0												
Equipment	0												
Monitoring	0												
Expend Total:	2,525,000	30,000		120,000	1,575,000	200,000	200,000	200,000	200,000	0	0	0	0
Revenues	Total	To Date	Carryover	FY14	FY15	FY16	FY17	FY18	FY19	FY20	FY21	FY22	FY23
TIF	2,300,000	30,000	1,150,000	120,000	200,000	200,000	200,000	200,000	200,000				
Utilities Fees	225,000				225,000								
Revenue Total:	2,525,000	30,000	1,150,000	120,000	425,000	200,000	200,000	200,000	200,000	0	0	0	0

October 2014 – Once comments from the different County departments were provided to the engineering consultant, Community Development staff and Kimley-Horn's project manager met with the property owners adjacent to the project to share with them the 30% plans and collect their feedback. These meetings with the property and business owners provided valuable information regarding their operations as they need to be taken into account when proposing the restructuration of driveway accesses to address safety concerns as required by the Land Development Code. Adjacent property owners were very energetic expressing their support towards the project and reiterating how much needed the sewer improvements are.

December 2014 – Conceptual drawings reflecting the improvements proposed in the 30% Design plans were presented to the Port Salerno NAC. Community members supported the project and requested staff to study the possibility to include more on-street parking.

March 2015 - 60% Roadway Design Plans were submitted by the engineering consultant for County review.

May 2015 - Review comments on the 60% design plans were provided to Kimley-Horn from the Engineering, Utilities and Community Development Department. The consultant will be meeting with staff to address those comments before moving forward with the development of the final design plans. Additional meetings with adjacent property and business owners will be scheduled to make sure they are fully aware of the proposed improvements and are able to provide any additional comments as they consider necessary.

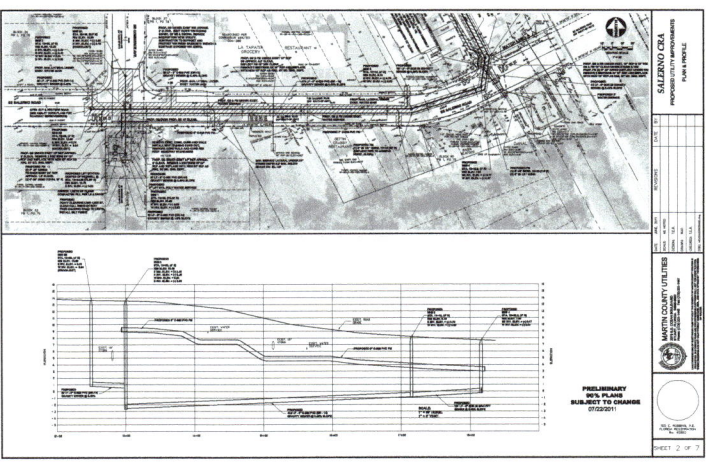

Left Top: *The route for the first phase of the Salerno Sewer Project maximizes the number of existing commercial developments that can convert from septic to sewer.*

Left Bottom: *The proposed route captures the highest taxable values per acre in the zoning overlay. These are the most productive properties, and have the best opportunity to increase in productivity once connected to public utilities.*

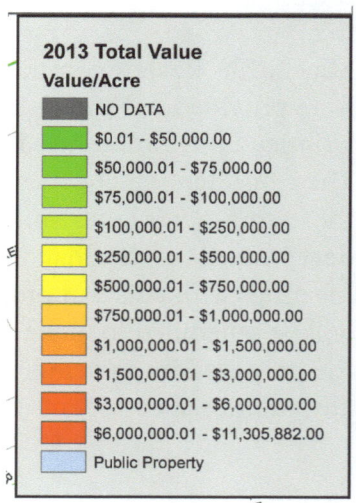

2013 Total Value
Value/Acre

■	NO DATA
■	$0.01 - $50,000.00
■	$50,000.01 - $75,000.00
■	$75,000.01 - $100,000.00
■	$100,000.01 - $250,000.00
■	$250,000.01 - $500,000.00
■	$500,000.01 - $750,000.00
■	$750,000.01 - $1,000,000.00
■	$1,000,000.01 - $1,500,000.00
■	$1,500,000.01 - $3,000,000.00
■	$3,000,000.01 - $6,000,000.00
■	$6,000,000.01 - $11,305,882.00
■	Public Property

Maximizing the Return on Investment

The goal of the Community Redevelopment Plan is to increase the value of properties within the redevelopment areas. To assist in this goal, a Community Redevelopment Plan is adopted to memorialize the community vision, and funding through Tax Increment Financing (TIF) to invest in this vision.

The routing of the first phase of sewer was based on the access to the existing forcemain on Dixie Highway, the placement of the lifts station to maximize its use and reach, and the ability to connect the maximum amount of existing developments to public utilities. The placement of the lift station is proposed in the unopened right of way of Commerce Avenue, and the route along Railway Avenue and along Salerno Road maximized these goals.

Staff also reviewed the taxable value per acre as reported by the Martin County Property Appraiser for these existing development parcels. The heat maps

to the left show the current value per acre, and the concentration of value. These properties have gradually increased in value since the adoption of the CRA, which has contributed to the Tax Increment Financing. The lower value properties along this route currently have very limited commercial development potential, which would change with the availability of public utilities.

In additional to the fiscal benefits of this project, there are several significant environmental benefits to the route of these utilities. Railway Avenue and Salerno Road include a variety of commercial businesses, including restaurants, which are operating on aging septic systems. There has already been at least one report of a failed system that resulted in a direct discharge into the Manatee Pocket. To reduce the pollution into the estuary, it is critical that these existing commercial properties connect to public utilities. As seen with the installation of sewer in the North River Shores neighborhood, the septic to sewer conversion results in immediate reductions of pollution into our estuaries.

21/09/2004

Implementation

Incremental Implementation

The Community Redevelopment Plan establishes a long term community vision for the future of the redevelopment area. The Community Development Department seeks opportunities to advance this vision with each capital investment through adaptive innovation. This lean approach to infrastructure supports the implementation of the community vision incrementally over time.

Stormwater Retrofits

Martin County is a leader in stormwater management projects that protect our estuaries, and the County has invested heavily within the Port Salerno Community Redevelopment Area. The Salerno Creek Retrofit is included in the Community Redevelopment Plan which provides water quality and flood protection to this area of Salerno Road.

The County has also constructed several stormwater management areas adjacent to Salerno Road to treat the run-off of this road. In addition to the water quality benefits, these areas contribute to the open space network.

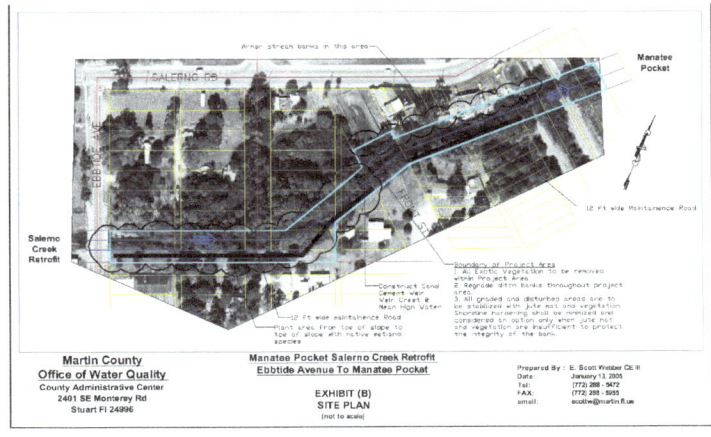

Salerno Foot Bridge

In the summer of 2010, the Martin County Engineering Department was forced to close the footbridge in Port Salerno due to structural failure. Citizens appealed to the Community Redevelopment Agency to find a way to re-open this pedestrian connection. The Agency worked with the Engineering Department to find a quick solution to re-open the bridge.

The Community Redevelopment Agency acquired, through the County's Engineering Department, a used foot bridge, which was salvaged, restored, and moved to Railway Avenue. This re-use saved the CRA over $30,000 and prevented almost 1 ton of steel from being added to the scrap yard.

In addition to the bridge, the CRA enhanced the pathway by carrying the character of the Manatee Pocket Walk across Dixie Highway. Upgraded fencing and landscaping were installed with pavers to further beautify the area.

Gateway: *The Salerno Footbridge was one of the best kept secrets along the Manatee Creek and adjacent to Salerno Road*

Commerce Avenue Demonstration Project

The success of several locally owned businesses in the Port Salerno Community Redevelopment Area has led to a greater need for public parking.

The Community Redevelopment Agency completed a preliminary analysis for the expansion of water of sewer in Port Salerno. The plan identified Commerce Avenue as a street that could be transformed to include on-street parking within the existing curb lines.

The Community Redevelopment Agency proposed a temporary demonstration project to add on-street parking to the west side of Commerce Avenue. This demonstration project was constructed at minimum cost, using temporary curbing and striping.

in collaboration with the paving needs of the County, the CRA was able to implement the vision at no additional cost to the County.

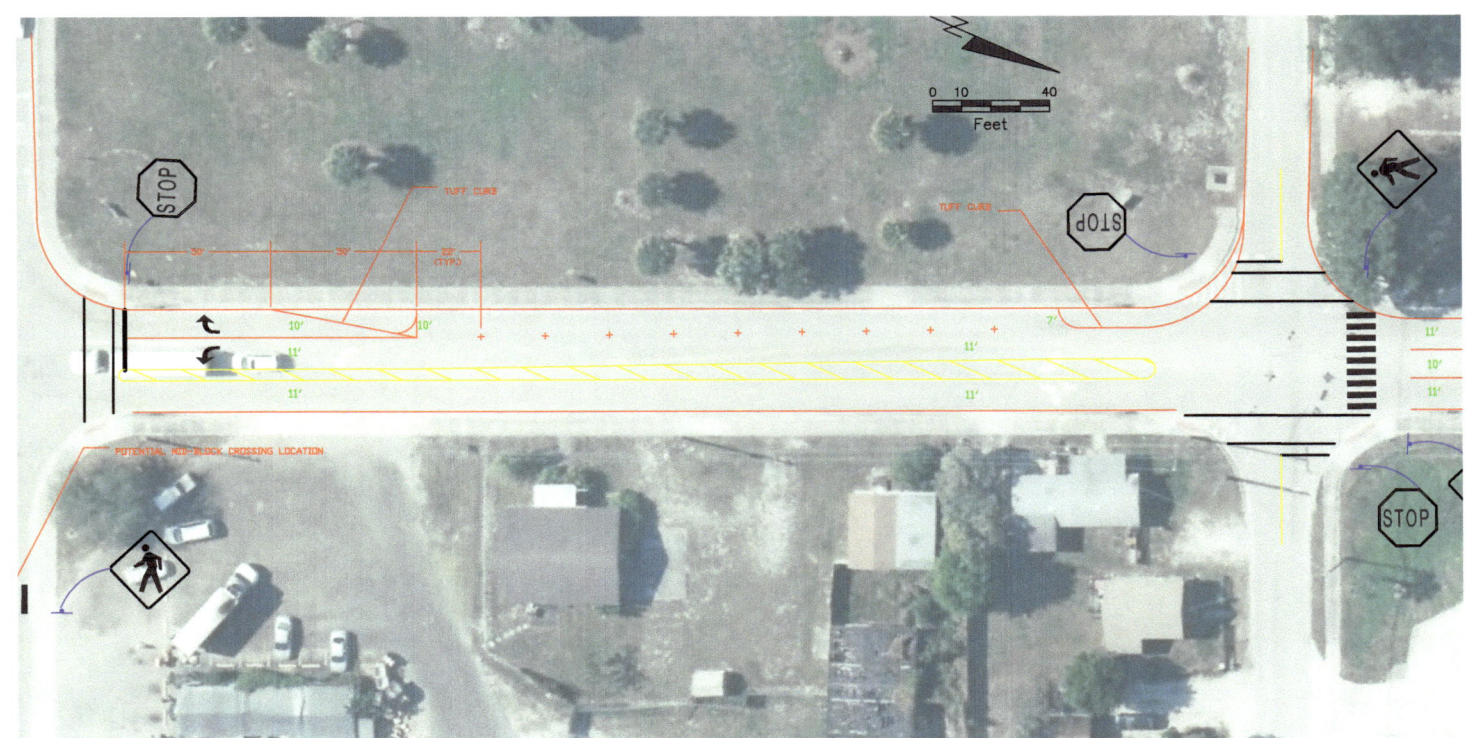